CONFLICT NEGOTIATION

John L. Lund, D.Ed.
Robert E. Lund, J.D.

The Communications Company

CONFLICT NEGOTIATION

*"Not all conflicts are resolved, but they can **all** be managed."*

Dr. John Lund

Copyright 2002 by
**John L. Lund D.Ed
Robert E. Lund J.D.**
All Rights Reserved

Art Work and Graphic Design
Nicole Lund
Printing & Communications Consultation
Russ Leseberg

Published by
The Communications Company
July 2002
For permission to copy any part of this publication contact:
drlund@drlund.com

ISBN 1-891114-01-8

Conflict Negotiation

The inability to resolve conflicts in healthy ways has been identified by John Gottman in his book, *Why Marriages Succeed or Fail*, as the single greatest factor leading to divorce and unhappy marriages. Somewhere between the marriage altar and the divorce court nearly half of all marital ships sink. It is not the pounding waves nor the external pressures which bring about this tragedy. It is the inability of the crew to steer the ship or even agree as to where it ought to be going, that creates havoc. It is the shipmates and their lack of knowledge, skills and cooperation which doom the vessel to wreck upon the shoals of misery and divorce. The disaster was brought about by internal strife and bickering. They faltered because they could not steer the ship on a mutually sustainable course after they had boarded the nuptial craft.

Common Consent

It was common consent that brought a man and a woman to the marriage altar. The agreement to be married was not forced upon either party. The decision was made by the free will of two people who agreed to sail together though life. By its very nature marriage is a relationship of equals which requires that the opinions of each party to the marriage be respected. The agreement to marry was itself a negotiation.

Marriage is a sharing of two lives and of two opinions that will impact upon a family and a nation. Negotiation is a process of coming to an agreement. How the agreement is reached, or

the process, is as important as the outcome. The means are as vital as the end. It is not enough to agree. It must be an agreement each can support with an enthusiastic attitude. Negotiation cannot be about winning or losing. It must be about sharing.

Reluctant acquiescence that harbors resentment for the sake of temporary peace is destructive to the relationship. Resentment is the feeling one experiences when he or she feels unfairly treated or "taken advantage of." Resentment and love dwell in opposite corners of the heart.

An agreement which cannot be sustained by both parties with a positive attitude is only a lull in the storm. The unresolved conflict will simply become the eye of a hurricane until the winds of the next conflict capsize their boat.

Men and women are different and distinct and their needs must be met in very unique ways. Loving and being loved and the behaviors that represent them are interpreted differently by the male and female. However, there are principles of interaction which can allow negotiation and sharing to take place in a loving environment. The principles of interaction become the rules of engagement. These will be the rules both parties agree to use when negotiating:

Rule # 1   Both parties will support the negotiated agreement with an enthusiastic attitude.

Rule # 2   Both parties will agree to negotiate only when they are in positive emotional control of themselves.

Rule # 3   Respect and equality will be reflected in the communication process.

Most people grow up in a family where they learn how to fight, quarrel, and be aggressive or defensive. They do not learn how to negotiate with respect and as an equal. For thousands of years, mankind has attempted to resolve conflicts by war, aggression and conquest.

How men and women approach each other is crucial to any subsequent negotiation. The latest research into brain-wiring differences between men and women demonstrates some amazing insights, which go against commonly held opinions. For example, most men avoid conflict and emotionally withdraw when confronted.

Only in a climate of respect and equality where both parties feel emotionally safe can lasting agreements survive. Divorce and unhappy marriages are a testimony of what is not working. The principles in this book work. They are, however, skill based and require practice. It is not enough to know about them. They must be practiced and applied. An important part of negotiating conflict is respecting the other parties in the way one deals with them. People need to love and be loved in the process. How one negotiates should contribute to feelings of love and not detract from the relationship. This is why it is imperative that men and women "be in emotional control" when they approach negotiation. Not only should negotiation begin with positive emotions, it should be conducted in a spirit of love, respect and equality.

It's
OK
to have conflicting points of view!

In fact...
Conflict is the normal and natural result of differing opinions.

Conflict is not inherently bad. Growth is often the product of a conflict of opinions.

Contention is different than conflict. Contention involves an unhealthy aggressiveness and a spirit of competition, rather than a spirit of cooperation.

HOW to or HOW NOT to...
resolve conflict is the issue.

In negotiating through a conflict, attitude is very important. Remember, the objective is not to win an argument. It is to understand the other person's point of view, explain your own position, explore mutually acceptable options and come to an agreement you can both support with a positive attitude. Maybe you have to agree to disagree and take turns.

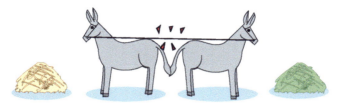

Negotiation is not about competition

Negotiation is about cooperation

Being stubborn, like a mule, means the person lacks willingness and the spirit of cooperation necessary for healthy negotiation.

HOW NOT to...

Don't run from conflict

Don't pretend there is no "real" problem

Don't get angry

Don't strike out

In fact...
Leave negative emotion out of it!

HOW NOT to...

Don't become verbally abusive

Don't name call

Don't attack self-worth

Never resort to physical abuse!

There can be no tolerance for hitting, kicking, pinching, or any unwanted physical touching, grabbing, or holding on to a person against his or her will. It is physical abuse and it is against the law.

When someone is physically abusive, call 911 and report him or her to the police.

"It's all your fault!"

Runnning Away

Physical Abuse

!@#$@&#$!&

Ignoring

Anger

Blame

"You are an idiot!"

"You never do anything right!"

Contention

Verbal Abuse

- Criticizing without permission
- Fault finding
- Complaining
- Name calling
- Blaming

Conflict Negotiation

fails when people lack the willingness, the courage, the knowledge, or the proper skills. Developing the communication skills to focus on issues of conflict and doing so with positive emotions is the objective.

Learning how to communicate with a positive attitude while negotiating is as easy as remembering the anagram Bingo.

Be in emotional control

Identify one issue

Negotiate

Generate a solution

Obligate yourself

e in emotional control

Communication is the responsiblity of both the message sender (Speaker) and the Listener because . . .

. . . communication is an exchange of understanding.

In order to keep the focus on the message, both the Speaker and the Listener need to be in emotional control.

e in emotional control

If someone is
defensive
it may be he or she is feeling
attacked

Even if you don't think you
are attacking the other person

Be in emotional control

Don't try to resolve a conflict when you or the other person is angry or upset.
WHY?
Because anger will escalate negativity into attack and counter attack until both parties are defensive.

Be prepared to logically explain your concerns. No yelling, crying, swearing, physical or emotional intimidation.

e in emotional control

Time Out and Time In

Sometimes it is necessary to take a *Time Out* to regain emotional control. Go for a walk, count to 100, etc. Whether you need 15 minutes or an hour take time to reestablish positive emotional control. Whenever you take a *Time Out* always give the other party a *Time In*. The *Time In* is the time you will return to discuss the issue with a positive attitude.

e in emotional control

Most people grow up in a family where they learn how to fight, quarrel, be angry and express themselves with negative emotions. They do not learn how to communicate with a positive attitude.

e in emotional control

Some Do's and Don'ts:

- Choose a mutually agreeable time and place. You may have to leave the house, hire a baby sitter, or meet in the garage in the car.

- Be alone with the person. The sheer presence of others will shift the focus from the issue to self awareness. People become defensive when other people are around. (The exception is an agreed upon coach or third party.)

- Stay focussed on the issue or the behavior. Do not attack their self-worth. Separate the issue from their worth to you.

- Affirm their worth to you. Often your concerns involve a criticism of the other person's behavior. This means you are asking for a behavioral change. Even if you follow the above guidelines you may still encounter a degree of defensiveness.

- Since their defensiveness is a defense of their worth, why not address the issue of their worth directly. Staying in emotional control and affirming their worth to you will help you focus on your original concern and not side track the issue into a brawl of accusatory words about your worth or theirs.

Be in emotional control

A good way to practice communicating your feelings and ideas is to write them out in a letter and then read the letter to the other party.

e in emotional control

Whether it's anger, silence, or tearful whimpering, most people have not learned to honestly evaluate an issue by separating it from their EGO.

When a person is in emotional control he or she can evaluate an issue on its merits. Getting emotional not only detracts from one's ability to examine the issue it changes the focus of the conversation and invariably makes it a matter of value. The self-worth issue (EGO) takes over and now the argument focuses on whether a person is loved, valued, or appreciated.

Be in emotional control

Being in emotional control means no yelling, crying, swearing, physical nor emotional intimidation. It means you are prepared or will get yourself prepared to logically choose and discuss an issue where you have a conflicting point of view.

Each of you be prepared to identify one issue you would like to resolve. Let's start with some small ones and work up to world peace.

Identify one issue

Communication is an exchange of understanding
Warning !

There are two mistakes that most people make:

- They rush to achieve agreement before they achieve understanding.
- They get off track and lose focus of the issue.

This is a part of skill development. Don't be side-tracked into other issues and don't rush to agreement before you have achieved understanding.

STAY
ON
TRACK

Identify one issue

Before a conflict can be resolved the participants must agree upon what the issue to be resolved is.

There are three sets of communication skills necessary to resolve conflicts in healthy ways.

They are...
1. Content Communication: The Speaker's responsibility
2. Active Listening and Tellback: The Listener's responsibility
3. Negotiation: A shared responsibility

Identifying one issue and succeeding in an exchange of understanding requires the Speaker or message-sender to be a Content Communicator and the Listener to be an Active Listener and to give "Tellback."

Identify one issue

For the Speaker to be a Content Communicator means he or she is required to say what he or she means and mean what he or she is saying. It cannot be cruel, brutal or delivered in an unkind manner. It can be honest and direct and focused on the issue. The message sender cannot expect the Listener to read minds, facial expressions or intonations of voice. There can be no hint dropping, sarcasm or indirect forms of communication.

Identify one issue

All frustration comes from unmet expectations. The more clearly you can identify your concern and translate it into a concrete measurable behavior, the more likely it is that your expectation can be met.

"I'm not happy," "I need you to do more," "You are not treating me right" are all examples of poorly communicated expectations.

Here are some examples of clearly content communicated expectations:

"I would appreciate it if you would bring me a single red rose once a month for no other reason than you love me."

"It would mean a lot to me if you would make sure I always had at least one dress shirt ironed and pressed in my closet."

"In public, I would like you not to contradict me when I am telling a story. Let me be responsible for my words. If I am wrong I will apologize."

Identify one issue

The Active Listening Skill requres the Listener to

Stop talking

Look at the person who is talking

Listen with the intent to understand

Identify one issue

The Skill of Tellback

Tellback is repeating back the information you received. Tellback is not feedback. Feedback involves giving your opinion. Tellback is also known as Repeat Back or Reflective Listening. It is simply repeating back what you heard, or paraphrasing it.

Examples of Tellback are...
"So what I heard you say is. . . "
or
"Your issues seem to be. . . "

Some people find it helpful to take notes.

Identify one issue

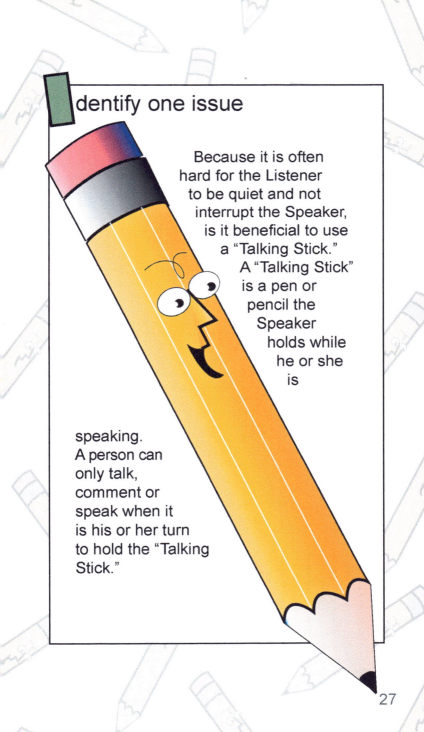

Because it is often hard for the Listener to be quiet and not interrupt the Speaker, is it beneficial to use a "Talking Stick." A "Talking Stick" is a pen or pencil the Speaker holds while he or she is speaking. A person can only talk, comment or speak when it is his or her turn to hold the "Talking Stick."

Identify one issue

Whether it is riding a bike, Content Communicating, Active Listening, or Tellback, it takes practice to develop the skill.

Let's Practice !

Identify one issue

What items would you truly like to negotiate in your relationship? Potential areas for conflict resolution could include matters relating to:

- Children
- Finances
- Religion
- Human Intimacy
- Entertainment
- Friends
- In-laws
- Criticisms
- Behavioral Traits
- Household Chores

Each of you identify one issue you would like to resolve

Remember, on some issues you may never agree. Some issues may have to be postponed. Work on the areas you are both willing to explore. One issue at a time, please.

Identify one issue

Flip a coin to see whose topic will be discussed first. If **Person A** wins the toss he or she will go first. Next time **Person B's** issue will be discussed.

30

Identify one issue

Person A is the Speaker with two minutes to express a point of view without interruption. Remember the Speaker is to be a Content Communicator. This means he or she is to communicate clearly in a positive way.

Person B is the Active Listener. It is the Active Listener's responsibility to do the following:

  Stop talking

 Look at the person who is talking

 Listen with the intent to understand

Identify one issue

Go ahead. **Person A** is to talk for two minutes on his or her chosen topic or about grounding teenagers for breaking family rules. Set a timer or look at a watch. Go!

Remember **Person A** is to use a pen or a pencil as a talking stick.

Identify one issue

At the conclusion of two minutes, **Person A** gives the Talking Stick to **Person B**.

The Active Listener *(Person B)* is to give Tellback to the Speaker *(Person A)*.

Remember Tellback is paraphrasing the information you received.
"So what I heard you say is this..."

Identify one issue

Confirmation

Give the Talking Stick back to **Person A**, the original Speaker. **Person A** is to confirm he or she has been understood. "Yes, that is what I said." If the Speaker does not feel understood he or she needs to clarify his or her position.

A successful exchange of understanding **does not mean agreement**. It means you have communicated your opinion.

Identify one issue

Reverse Roles

Now reverse roles...
Person B has the Talking Stick and two minutes to communicate his or her issue or about grounding teenagers for breaking family rules. **Person A** is now the Active Listener. Stop, look, and listen. After two minutes of listening, the Listener gives only Tellback by reflecting the concerns of **Person B**. This time **Person B** confirms he or she has been understood.

Identify one issue

You haven't negotiated yet, but you have achieved
Understanding

No one is expecting perfection. There will be mistakes and challenges until you have practiced the skills enough to become completely familiar with the process.

36

Identify one issue

ASSIGNMENT

Complete at least three successful active listening sessions.

The topic for practice session # 1 was ***Person A's*** issue or "Do you feel grounding a teenager for breaking family rules is necessary?"

The topic for practice session # 2 could be ***Person B's*** issue or "Where would you like to go on your next vacation and why?"

The topic for practice session # 3 could be "Should husbands and wives have separate checking accounts? What are the advantages or disadvantages?"

Identify one issue

Sometimes it is helpful to have a third party
Coach

Identify one issue

- The Coach is to see the rules of engagement are strictly enforced.
- The Speaker has the Talking Stick.
- The Active Listener has the responsibility to stop talking, look at the Speaker, and listen with the intent to understand.
- When the Speaker is finished, the Listener receives the Talking Stick and gives Tellback. There is no debate, nor feedback. There is only Tellback.
- The Speaker takes back the Talking Stick and confirms he or she has been understood.

Understanding the Speaker is the objective.

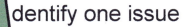
Identify one issue

ASSIGNMENT
Involve a third party

Each member of the family could take a turn as a...

- Message Sender, who as the Speaker is to be a Content Communicator.
- An Active Listener, who is to Stop, Look, and Listen for understanding. The next skill of the Active Listener is to give Tellback.
- Coach, who is to see these rules of communication are followed.

Identify one issue

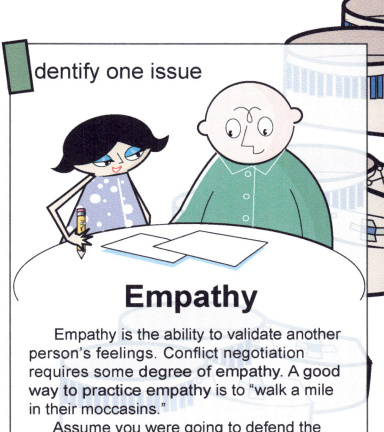

Empathy

Empathy is the ability to validate another person's feelings. Conflict negotiation requires some degree of empathy. A good way to practice empathy is to "walk a mile in their moccasins."

Assume you were going to defend the other person's point of view. Remove any personal opinions or negative feelings. Focus on their issue. Why would they feel the way they do? When you understand their feelings and not just their words you have empathy.

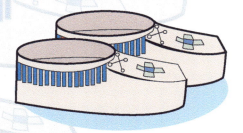

Identify one issue

Empathy is a learned behavior. Communicating so that you are understood is also a learned behavior.

Whether as serious as family finances or as benign as deciding on where to go for dinner, the tools of empathy and understanding can be an important part of the process of negotiation.

Identify one issue

Let's role play an empathy, "walk a mile in their moccasins" experience.

Not feeling appreciated seems to be an issue about which most people have strong feelings.

1. *Person A*, using the Talking Stick, express your point of view on "Why I don't feel appreciated."
2. *Person B* actively listen and give not only Tellback, but "Feelback" (empathy).

Feelback is an invented term which means to reflect not just the words, but the feelings of the other person. Lower your tone of voice closer to a whisper and sincerely respond. Remember this is a new skill for most people, especially men, and may feel awkward, forced, phoney, or unnatural. Try it anyway.

3. *Person A*, using the Talking Stick, confirms he or she has been understood.
4. If *Person A* believes his or her feelings were not understood, repeat the process.
5. Now reverse roles with *Person B* using the Talking Stick and *Person A* giving Tellback and Feelback. *Person B* confirms that he or she has been understood.

Identify one issue

ASSIGNMENT
Involve a third party

With three people, complete three successful Active Listening sessions...

The topic for session # 1 could be "How would you feel about moving the driving age for teenagers to 18 instead of 16 and why?"

The topic for session # 2 could be
"My opinion of an ideal wife is . . ."
"My opinion of an ideal mother is . . ."
"My opinion of an ideal daughter is . . ."

The topic for session # 3 could be
"My opinion of an ideal husband is . . ."
"My opinion of an ideal father is . . ."
"My opinion of an ideal son is . . ."

Identify one issue

When you have successfully completed this assignment, it means you have the skill of an

Active Listener

Congratulations !

Negotiate

Conflict Negotiation is sometimes conflict management which means you agree to disagree without being disagreeable. This encompasses three sets of communication skills. The first set of skills includes Content Communication. The second skill set requires Active Listening and Tellback, which you have now practiced.

The third set of skills involves the ability to negotiate and reach an agreement with a positive attitude.

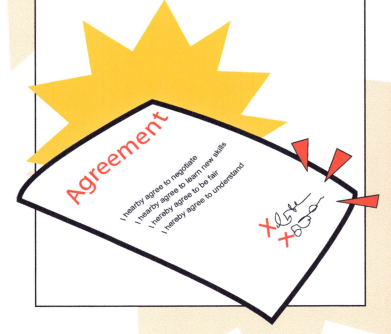

Negotiate

What is negotiation?

Negotiation begins when you are open to alternatives in addition to your own opinions.

egotiate

The difference between a **negotiation** and an **argument** is the **willingness** to respect a different point of view and to allow for fairness in coming to a mutually acceptable agreement.

The Keys to Successful Negotiation

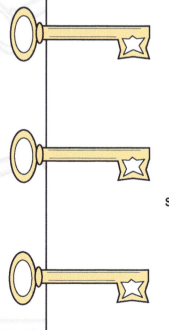

The first key is fairness, a willingness to give and take.

The second key to successful negotiation is that both parties walk away from the agreement with something important to each of them.

The third key is a willingness to support the decision with a good attitude.

 egotiate

Negotiation is a process.

How you come to agreement is as important as the outcome.

Negotiation is the process of coming to an agreement. Negotiation is a shared responsibility.

 egotiate

LET'S PRACTICE CONFLICT MANAGEMENT

Checklist for a healthy Conflict Management Session

Agree to meet at a time and place where the two of you can be alone.

We have agreed to meet at: _____ am/pm

at the following place:

_____

Let's assume you have decided to meet at 9:00 pm in the car in the garage.

51

egotiate

You are both in emotional control and prepared to logically explain your points of view.

The identified issue is this: You have received $10,000 of unexpected income. What will you do with the money?

• The Speaker will be a Content Communicator using the Talking Stick.

• The Listener will be an Active Listener. He or she will **Stop**, **Look**, and **Listen** for understanding. He or she will take notes if necessary.

• After Tellback and Confirmation of Understanding, record the opinion of *Person A*. What is *Person A's* opinion of how to spend the $10,000?

_____
_____
_____
_____
_____
_____
_____

 egotiate

Time to switch roles !

Person B is the Content Communicator and has the Talking Stick.

Person A is now the Active Listener and gives Tellback to **Person B** when he or she is finished.

Person B confirms he or she has been understood.

What is **Person B's** opinion of how to spend the $10,000 of unexpected income?

_____
_____
_____
_____
_____
_____
_____
_____

Negotiate

Negotiation is about looking for mutually acceptable alternatives.
Person A's opinion is one option.
Person B's opinion is a second option.

Brainstorming is a way to explore mutually acceptable alternatives.

The rules for BRAINSTORMING are simple. Think and write down as many alternatives as you can. No negativism. During the brainstorming session, do not reject any idea nor make any negative comments. This is the time to explore options. What else might you do with the $10,000?

Brainstorming options:

_____
_____
_____
_____
_____
_____
_____
_____

 egotiate

Not all decisions can be made in a single session. Indeed it would not be wise to force a decision because of time. After a good brainstorming session take a break. Sleep on it and set a time to get back together unless you both feel good about an obvious option.

egotiate

When you can't agree you have options

You can agree to disagree, postpone any decisions or say,

"Let's take turns!"

enerate a solution

Here are some things to think about when looking for a solution:

CHOICES

- Choose an option you can both support.
- Defer to the one for whom it matters most.
- Agree to disagree.
- Take turns (Meaning this time you will do it one way and another time you will do it another way).
- Remember, you are never expected to agree to anything illegal, immoral, or against your basic core values.

enerate a solution

Honestly look at each option.
Ask yourself two questions:
1. Will doing this help me become my best self?
2. Will doing this help our relationship?

Remember the objective is a mutual agreement you can both support with a great attitude.
If you can't agree, then agree to disagree and split the money.

G enerate a solution

An important part of negotiation is separating one's EGO from the ISSUE. It is not about being right or winning. It is about coming to a mutual agreement.

What did the two of you decide to do with the $10,000 of unexpected income? What was the agreed upon solution that was generated by the negotiation process?

We agreed to:

_____
_____
_____
_____
_____
_____
_____
_____
_____
_____

bligate yourself

Commit to your best efforts to make the agreed upon solution work.

It is now about unity. Coming to common consent with a positive attitude requires a willingness to support and sustain the agreement and enthusiastically obligate yourself to follow through with its terms and conditions.

Obligate yourself

Obligating yourself may be the most important part of the negotiation process.

Looking for options, discussing alternatives, and generating a mutually agreeable solution was part of the decision making process.

The time for brainstorming, exploring options and debating is over. It is now time to sustain the agreed upon solution.

Unity is now more important than rehashing differences.

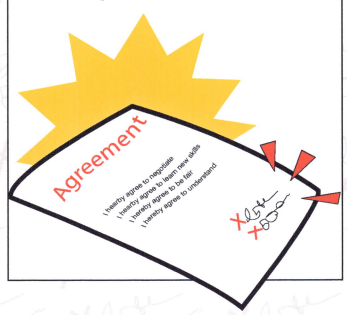

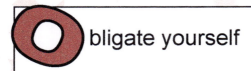
Obligate yourself

Obligating yourself is about implementing the agreed upon solution. Resentment or reluctant acquiescence means you have failed to obligate yourself to a positive supportive role. Once you have signed an agreement and then honored with integrity its terms and conditions, you have succeeded in
Negotiating a Conflict in a Healthy Way.

Set a specific time to review your decision in the future.

Obligate yourself

Continue to practice on the following pages the issues the two of you have raised. You now possess the knowledge and the skills to resolve conflicts in healthy ways. It is now up to you to provide the willingness to make it happen.

Be in emotional control

We have agreed to meet at: _____ am/pm

at the following place: _____

Identify one issue

The identified issue is...

_____

Negotiate

Person A's opinion: _____

_____

Person B's opinion: _____

_____

Brainstorming options: _____

_____

_____

_____

Generate a solution

We have agreed to... _____

_____

Obligate yourself

I commit to give my best efforts to support and sustain our agreed upon solution.

We will meet to review our agreement on... _____

Sign: _____ Sign: _____

Conflict Negotiaion Worksheet

Be in emotional control

We have agreed to meet at: _____ am/pm

at the following place: _____

Identify one issue

The identified issue is...

_____

Negotiate

Person A's opinion: _____

_____

Person B's opinion: _____

_____

Brainstorming options: _____

_____

_____

_____

Generate a solution

We have agreed to... _____

_____

Obligate yourself

I commit to give my best efforts to support and sustain
our agreed upon solution.

We will meet to review our agreement on... _____

Sign: _____ Sign: _____

Conflict Negotiaion Worksheet